CONTENTS

Chapter 1 Where Did I Go Wrong? I Was Just Trying to Help

A *group of managers had a project to get done for their boss. They met and decided to divide up the work and get it done by the end of the month. Mary asked if they needed a leader.*

"Why?" Bill responded. "We're all leaders and know what we need to do. We'll get the job done. We don't need the formality of a leader." One week into the project Mary was concerned because nothing seemed to be getting done. It had been a busy week at work and everyone promised they would try harder the following week. The second week, nothing was done again. This time Mary took control and began acting like a leader. She contacted each team member privately and said, "Please don't take this the wrong way, but I

just want to make sure we get the project done. I'm not trying to be a boss or anything." Everyone said not to worry. They were fine with Mary emerging as the leader and taking control to get the project done. As the deadline approached, Bill continued to have conflicts that interfered with him getting his portion done. Mary sent an e-mail to the group reminding them the deadline was approaching and a lot of work still needed to be done. Bill took

offense with the e-mail and shot back his own e-mail saying he said he would get his portion done and to stop pestering him. Nobody else commented. Finally the deadline arrived, Bill's portion was not done, and Mary completed it so they could meet the boss's deadline. The team met and Bill told Mary he didn't appreciate her doing his portion, as it made him look bad. Mary replied, "But we had a deadline for the boss and you still did not have your portion completed. What were we supposed to do?"
Bill shouted back, "Who put you in charge anyway? I thought this was a team and didn't need a leader?"
"Fine, next time I'll just let the project not get done," said Mary.
Bill replied, "It would have gotten done." "How?" Mary asked. "You never did your portion. How would it have gotten done without your key section?"
"I told you I was busy," Bill shouted back. "Don't you listen to anything I say?" Nobody from the rest of the team said
anything.

Me?

Finally Sue said, "Well Mary, maybe Bill has a point. You're not our boss. Who are you to criticize Bill?"
Mary felt hurt, frustrated, and like she was a scapegoat for the groups problems.

The Dynamics of Bullying

It is not clear if bullying is on the rise or we are just looking at it more closely. Bullying is defined as a set of antisocial behavior that being in childhood and manifest differently in boys vs. girls. Boys tend to display physical aggression, while girls typically engage in relational types of aggression such as gossip or excluding other girls from situations (Leff 2006, 2007). Leff found bullying behaviors manifested in girls as young as nine (9) years old in schools, playgrounds, and other social situations. There are many theories for why bullying exists in adults who are nurses, but it has reached such epidemic proportions that the Joint Commission developed standards to address it (Center for American Nurses, 2008).

Experienced nurses complain that they do not have the time or patience to train young nurses, who should have been properly trained in nursing school, as some senior nurses like to point out that they were. Novice nurses report experiencing resistance to teach, poor attitude, impatience, intimidation, rude behaviors, and frustration from senior nurses when they ask them for assistance. Younger nurses say that senior nurses make them feel stupid when they ask a question, that they are bothering the busy senior nurses, and that they should figure out things on their own. What is most concerning is the potential impact on patient safety when a young nurse feels intimidated to ask a question, or feels her concerns about a patient's condition are ignored. Young nurses need guidance and emotional support if they are to provide appropriate, safe, quality care.

Rosenblooth (1994) an executive in the travel industry wrote a book years ago called, *The Customer Comes Second*. Rosenblooth suggested that the key to exceptional customer service begins with employee's being treated right, which

Me?

they then pass along to the customer. Bullying can become endemic to a culture as one generation of bullied nurses takes the same approach in orienting the next generation of nurses. Grant (2013; 2013, April) suggested that organizations take on a pattern of behaviors. Some organizations have a *giver* mentality, while others are more *takers*. The *taker* organization has a greater focus on individual achievement, and encourages competition. These organizations are prone to bullying type behaviors, whereas the *giver* organizations or more support of employees and co-workers.

Lateral Violence

Bullying has also been described as lateral violence (Sheridan-Leos, 2008). Lateral violence is generally defined as covert or overt actions targeting another individual. Covert behaviors may be unintentional, secret, and something the perpetrator is so used to doing they don't even realize the harmful effects. Overt lateral violence is purposeful, face-to-face, and intended to harm someone, usually targeting psychological damage. Later in this chapter we discuss rumors, gossip, and the fact that they are rooted in negative feelings about the victim. Lateral violence is violence that occurs between nurses at the same level, unlike scapegoating, which also manifests between nurses and management; physicians; and assistive personnel.

Sheridan-Leos (2008, p. 401) described the various forms of lateral violence as:

• Nonverbal cues (covert & overt): Raising eyebrows, rolling eyes, or making faces in reply to a question.
• Verbal remarks (overt): Snide, rude, and demeaning comments; and abrupt responses to honest questions.
• Actions (overt): Actions that undermine the victim's ability to perform in the healthcare setting (e.g., hiding or hording limited patient care items from other nurses). Not being available to help the other nurse with difficult care issues. Refusing or continually being too busy to help during difficult care issues.
• Withholding information (covert & overt): The information can be about a

Me?

patient or a procedure (e.g., deliberately not telling another nurse important details of a patients condition).
• Purposefully sabotaging behaviors (overt): This may place the other nurse in a negative situation and place patients at a risk for injury.
• Group infighting (overt): Nurses often develop social cliques and exclude other staff members.
• Scapegoating (overt): Blaming negative outcomes on one identified nurse.
• Passive-aggressive behavior (overt): Failure to resolve conflicts directly. Complaining to others about a person but not speaking directly to that person.
• Broken confidences & not respecting privacy (covert): These behaviors include spreading rumors, gossiping, and sharing confidential information that could have a negative impact on someone's reputation.

The Foundations of Lateral Violence

Many theories exist regarding the causes of lateral violence, bullying, and scapegoating behaviors including the oppressed-group model; gender theories; patterns of tough approaches; and culture, which are covered in the following sections.

Oppressed-Group Model

The theory behind this model is that oppressed groups tend to pass on the same behaviors to the next generation. This explains why someone who was abused as a child, would abuse their own children or why we often find ourselves as parents doing the same behaviors toward our children that we hated having done to us as a child. While some nurses may find this theory offensive, the fact remains that we have had multiple generations of oppressed nurses mistreating the next generation of nurses.

Nurses are vulnerable to feeling like they are not listened to by their leaders, are abused by their co-workers, and lack autonomy. Feeling powerless to address these larger issues some nurses internalize their frustrations becoming depressed or exhibiting other mental and physical symptoms. Other nurses may react

Me?

outwardly by lashing out at their peers including novice nurses and co-workers (Sheridan-Leos, 2008).

Gender Theory

Nurses are still predominantly women (93%) and the profession tends to take on a female-like personality. Nursing is largely controlled by physicians and administrators who come from male dominant cultures. The significance is that women are more likely to outwardly express their emotions or suppress their feelings and internalize their anger. Internalizing anger and frustration eventually leads to an explosion of pent up anger, which may manifest as lateral violence (Sheridan-Leos, 2008).

Patterns of Tough Approaches

Nursing is not the only profession that treats its young in a tough manner. Hoopes (2003) suggested that the entire 20th century of management theory was built on military and slavery models which clearly had oppressive approaches toward their employees. Nursing can be a challenging and stressful profession however there is limited research to demonstrate that oppressive forms of orientation and daily peer interaction lead to healthy, effective outcomes in terms of patient safety, quality, and employee satisfaction. While the perpetrators may believe their approach is useful, it is rare to find a worker who says they are not being abused enough by their peers, because they find it motivating to be abused.

Cultural Impacts

Lateral violence can become endemic to a culture, much like the dynamics of an abused spouse who begins to believe that domestic violence is normal. Nurses who feel oppressed and powerless may unwittingly exert power over a co-worker and in the process feel some level of control over their own situation. Unfortunately staff can begin to believe that lateral violence is acceptable behavior when it become part of a unit's culture, *it's just how we behave.* Longo (2007) suggested changes need to take place from the very beginning of

Me?

enculturation, with new nurses in school. Generally, when nurses are in school they are treated in a more supported manner, taught to recognize lateral violence, and encouraged to address it when it occurs.

The Impact of Lateral Violence

The primary impact of lateral violence is psychological distress leading to job dissatisfaction, poor performance, and eventually to turnover. The psychological symptoms can include stress, depression, anxiety, low selfesteem, poor social skills, and posttraumatic stress disorder. Nurses may also exhibit physical symptoms, such as weight fluctuations, hypertension, palpitations, and bowel disorders. Ultimately the job dissatisfaction can lead to the nurse leaving the unit, the hospital, or even the profession of nursing (Sheridan-Leos, 2008).

The cost of nursing turnover is not just related to training new nurses. There is a larger impact in terms of the ability to recruit and retain nurses when an organization develops a reputation as a difficult place to work.

Rumors, Gossip, and Lateral Violence

Rumors and gossip are another form of lateral violence, which can be detrimental to the organizational culture. Often chronic complainers are the ones who spread rumors, gossip, and are abusive to other staff. The abuse of coworkers has been a problem in nursing for decades rising to the point where the Joint Commission wrote a standard around the issue of lateral violence in the workplace. Rumors and gossip are prevalent and dangerous in nursing organizations, yet received little attention in the literature until recently (Michelson & Mouly, 2000; Michelson & Mouly, 2002). The connection between rumors, gossip, and lateral violence is that there is usually a malicious foundation to spreading a rumor. People do not generally spread rumors about their friends, but think nothing of saying, *I don't know if this is true or not, but I heard Suzie…*

Me?

Rumors can become harmful to the organization when they convey inaccurate, hurtful information and innuendo, which can lower morale and undermine productivity. Rumors and gossip may also be used as a tactic in organizational politics when inaccurate information is transmitted knowingly to damage an opponent. Rumors tend to increase when employees have limited control over events, where there is a poor organizational climate, mistrust of formal communication lines, uncertainty about change, and high levels of competition (Michelson & Mouly, 2000; Michelson & Mouly, 2002).

Leaders can set the tone by addressing rumors and gossip through a no-tolerance policy built into the unit's code of conduct. Leaders should never accept that *Suzie is a good nurse, she just gossips a lot.* Gossip can be extremely damaging to employee morale and employees must be held accountable for their negative behavior.

Summary

In this chapter we began to explore the foundations of scapegoating behavior, which is grounded in a well meaning person who attempts to accomplish a task and is met by resistance, jealousy, and bullying behaviors. Scapegoating is a form of lateral violence and is often accompanied by rumors and gossip, which not only undermines the implementation of the project but can also have and impact on the credulity of the scapegoat. In the next chapter the topic of blame, leaderless groups, and the scapegoating phenomenon will be addressed.

Me?

Chapter 2 Why Does Someone Have to Take the Blame?

One of the true tests of scapegoating is the ability to recognize the problem before it becomes an emergency.

Arnold H. Glasgow

Work groups are often averse to
appointing a leader and mistakenly believe they have the right amount of
cohesion to perform as a *leaderless* team. It is not unusual to hear teams say,
we're all adults we don't need a bunch of rules. The initial enthusiasm is
often not enough to complete the work and it is common for an informal
leader to emerge and take charge, with the group's tacit approval. This well-
intentioned emerging leader merely wants to get the task completed and feels
they are helping the group by taking control. For a while this approach works
fine, until pushback occurs from one or several members of the group. The
emerged leader may be attacked and blamed for the group's difficulty. The
emerged leader's authority is questioned as the attack escalates. Suddenly, the
dialogue shifts from the group's inability to complete the task, to who put the
emerged leader in charge. As Mary discovered in our scenario, the real issue
was not Mary's role as the informal leader. The issue was why people were
not accountable for their commitment to completing what they said they
would do. The debate about Mary's leadership role diverts attention away
from the tasks at hand, and allows the group to avoid discussing the real
matter of why they did not live up to their promises to do their portion of the
project. This dynamic has been described as scapegoating and mobbing. A
review of the history of scapegoating and mobbing; dynamics behind it; and
suggestions for avoiding it will be explored in this chapter.

Background

In Leviticus 16 a ritual was identified where a goat was driven into the
wilderness to symbolically carry the

Me?

sins of the people (The Bible: Authorized King James Version, 2008).
Labeled as the *scapegoat*, this dynamic with the goat has been used to
describe any person, who is blamed or punished for the wrong doings of the
larger group. In general, by focusing attention on the scapegoat, the members
are distracted from the real causes of the problems. From a Christian
perspective Jesus was a scapegoat, who was driven from his homeland,
accepting the blame for the sins of those he left behind.

Westhues (2002) described

workplace mobbing as a form of social scapegoating, which has one beneficial effect of increasing group cohesion by rallying to blame the scapegoat. This phenomenon is a common occurrence among groups where avoiding
accountability leads to blaming someone for the group's failure.

Hertzberg did experiments in the Hawthorn Factory in the 1920's aimed at identifying what motivated employees (Bass, 1990). Probably the most famous result was the Hawthorne effect, where they found subjects improved their performance merely because someone was paying attention to them, not necessarily in response to the
experimenter manipulating some variable like the lighting, who they worked with, and rest breaks. This was the early evolution of research showing that employee performance is related to being involved, having a voice, and feeling they are appreciated by their leaders. Another disturbing experiment was the
introduction of a highly motivated and productive employee into the environment. Intuitively one would think they would motivate their fellow employees, yet in reality jealousy and resentment got in the way and co-workers tended to influence the highly motivated employee to perform at a lower level of productivity.

The jealousy and resentment of motivated employees may be some of the basis for scapegoating. Unfortunately, there are negative consequences to scapegoating, which we will discuss through a case scenario in the next section.

Me?

Scapegoating & the Group Project

Mary was assigned by her manager to work on a Shared Governance sub-team investigating the impact of nurse fatigue on patient errors. There were 12 people on the work group representing all sectors of the healthcare facility. Mary's boss, a nurse manager, came to the first meeting and assigned the group their task: To come up with a solution to the fatigue problem of nurses working 12-hour shifts. The nurse manager was only present for this first meeting and no formal leader was appointed. After two contentious meetings the group was stuck debating whether the problem was 12-hour shifts or faulty data collection regarding patient errors. Mary suggested the group needed direction and facilitation. Jane, a member of the group suggested that Mary serve as the leader of this project. A quick vote was taken and Mary was appointed the leader. Mary was very effective as the leader and the group began moving in the direction of looking at whether 12-hour shifts were the problem or whether it was the lack of rest breaks that led to the fatigue. A highly emotional debate occurred in which several members of the group argued that 12-hour shifts were never going to go away and that their unit was too busy to take breaks. Suddenly the debate shifted to Mary's role as group leader. Someone shouted out, "Who made you the boss anyway Mary? This is a shared governance team. Everyone is an equal. If administration wanted a leader they would have appointed one. I have a manager who is my boss and sets policy on my unit!" The remainder of the meeting was spent debating Mary's role.

Mary replied at one point, "I was only trying to help. The team elected me the leader." Jane replied, "Not everyone had a chance to vote, we never decided what the leader role would be, and we did not knew at the time that it would come down to this: the

elimination of 12-hour shifts."

Mary felt hurt, betrayed, and humiliated. She resigned as leader of the project. At that point the group tried to finish the project, but could never come to any conclusions.

I Was Only Trying to Help

Scapegoating is especially
disturbing for an over-achiever who sets out with the noble goal of trying to

Me?

improve a situation and suddenly finds themselves a target of politics, jealousy, and a confusing organizational dynamic. While it is easy to blame the formal leaders for this dynamic, it may be more complicated and harder to fix. Oshry (1994, 1996) suggested the role of middle level leaders is to push the tension in an organization and that it is unrealistic to think an organization can change without there being some tension and pushback. The greatest impact on change may be in middle management and through empowered staff. Giving staff the tools to understand and react to the dynamics of scapegoating and use it to their advantage is a compelling argument. One goal of leadership should be to create a safe environment where nurses at the staff level feel empowered to move along the performance continuum from low level to mid and high level change agents and formal leaders (Perrotto & Grossman, 2010). Nurses must have the necessary skills to deal with this subtle form of bullying that places the change agent in the position of being attacked by the group they are trying to change.

Scapegoats are often mid-level leaders who have a pattern of being high performers. Thus, they are called on to deal with administrative issues outside their formal job roles, or they volunteer to fill the void to lead projects. Mid-level leaders often function at a higher level because leaders at higher levels in the organization may be hesitant to take a stand on issues for fear of risking political repercussions for whatever decision they make. In turn, staff will turn to anyone they perceive to be in a position to help them in the absence of effective
leadership. This dynamic creates a ripple effect in the organization as the mid-level leader begins solving problems and creating solutions for day-to-day
operations. This may be the beginning of a dangerous mix of issues.

Directors and administrators often ask mid-level leaders for support, solutions, and to actually take the lead on projects. The formal leader may actually justify this as a form of *empowering* the next lower levels of the organization. However, when pushback from others manifests as attacking the mid-level

Me?

leader, the formal leader needs to step in to avoid the mid-level leader becoming the focus of scapegoating behavior.

Summary

In this chapter we began to explore why scapegoating occurs, the historical foundations of scapegoating behavior, and early experiments with scapegoating in the workplace. In the next chapter the topics of power, politics, mobbing, and scapegoating as a distraction to gain superiority will be explored.

Me?

Chapter 3 Let the Games Begin

When the messenger arrives and says 'Don't shoot the messenger,' it's a good idea to be prepared to shoot the messenger, just in case.

Howard Tayler

Don't Shoot the Messenger

Shooting the messenger is a metaphor that goes back to earlier times in history when information was delivered by a messenger sent to personally deliver information such as the war had been lost or someone had died. The Latin term *Ad Hominem* describes the concept of
insulting an opponent to invalidate their argument. We see this in politics regularly where an opponent's credibility is attacked by focusing on a character attack, to distract from the important message they are trying to convey: *He cheated on his wife, how can we believe anything he has to say about the war?*

Unfortunately, as we will see in this chapter, the concept of Ad Hominem works and thus an important message can get lost in the process. Shakespeare is often credited with popularizing the term, in his book about Henry IV, the King of England (Shakespeare, 2009). The King wanted to know how his son and brother were doing in the war, but also warned the messenger that the first one to bring unwelcome news would lose their position. What a tough position to be placed in. Today we talk about
transparency in organizations, and encourage people to speak up about safety and ethics violations. We have compliance offices, ethics hotlines, and laws to protect whistle blowers, yet we still find that 90% of whistle blowers get fired in the United States (Armstrong, 2002).

The issue here is organizational censorship of people who speak up. Rather than addressing the problems

Me?

organizations will create an environment of *silence* where employees know they will be targeted for termination (Hutchison, Vickers, & Jackson, 2006). The end result is the employee who speaks up is then labeled as the problem, targeted for bullying and eventually leaves or is fired (Hutchison, Vickers, & Jackson). Many organizations have multiple bullies, whose dysfunctional behavior can effect the entire organization leading to discontent and employee turnover, yet it is tolerated.

Scapegoating and Mobbing as a Social Phenomenon

Westhues (2002) described mobbing behavior as a sociological phenomenon in which the group attacks a member to maintain their own superiority. Mobbing is often a passive-aggressive act and serves the unconscious effect of detracting from the true mission of the group, while also absolving the other members of the group of their personal responsibility and accountability, as attention is drawn to attacking the victim. Westhues suggested this dynamic was more prevalent in environments where employee rights and hierarchy were the most structured, as there is little room for a formal assault on the victim.

Mobbing and scapegoating are quite similar in the attack on an innocent victim. Either approach serves one functional purpose of temporarily achieving group solidarity in uniting to attack the victim. The question remains whether it is the most functional approach in terms of long-term group cohesiveness and goal attainment. At its worst, mobbing and scapegoating become a collective effort to punish, humiliate, and eventually remove someone from a group who started out with the noble intentions of helping the group to be successful.

Mobbing is often a contagious process in which the stories about the scapegoat gain myth-like proportions as more individuals join the campaign, add to the stories, and embellish them. Eventually the hostility is seen as justified by the scapegoat's egregious actions and

Me?

the negative group behaviors are seen as justified. Eventually, most scapegoats succumb to the pressure and withdrawal from active participation or leave the group.

Mobbing is the larger social phenomenon in which peers single out a coworker for public humiliation, sexual harassment, verbal and emotional abuse, less desirable work assignments, and social isolation (Westhues, 2002). Scapegoating and mobbing behavior is often initiated by a person in power, such as a manager or administrator but can be common occurrences between co-workers as well.

There is little information and research regarding why people become the target of mobbing, however Westhues suggested that in most cases the target may be feared by the mobbing group because of their own less than ideal performance and lack of achievements. Targets of mobbing may also be those who have a relatively secure job, which in some way threatens the manager or coworkers. Workplace mobbing tends to occur in professional environments such as education, health care, union factories, and public service organizations
(Westheus). Gravois (2006) identified several cases of workplace mobbing within universities where victims of the violence and emotional abuse described it as a sudden onset of negative behaviors from peers.

Scapegoating in Healthcare

Healthcare is a prime environment for workplace mobbing and scapegoating (Westhues, 2002). The initial goal of mobbing is to psychologically damage the intended victim with the ultimate result of victimizing the person into quitting or leaving the position Mobbing becomes a necessary tactic because in general, the person is an average or high performer and in most cases legal or justifiable termination cannot be achieved
(Westhues; Gravois, 2006). Occasionally, the group will stop short of mobbing and promote scapegoating as an effective tool for eliminating the unwanted peer. In essence, workplace mobbing is nothing more than social out casting of a peer out

Me?
of fear and jealousy of their achievements and abilities.

Protection from the Mob

Loyalty to the mob is an essential function in organizations that unwittingly promote corruption and bullying. In the movie *The Godfather*, loyalty to the family was the number one priority. Covey (1990) suggested that gangs are often highly effective teams, even if their mission is not for the good of mankind. Lack of loyalty to the family, in *The Godfather* was seen as dishonorable behavior and grounds for serious
punishment.

Ed, a participant at one of our

workshops said he had read a book about the mafia and being a part of the group and it reminded him of when he worked in the Emergency Department (ED) prior to taking a director job. There was a group of nurses who were just like the mafia in the novel he read. If they didn't like you they ran you out of the ED. They would let you drown during busy times. They helped each other but nobody else and while they weren't helping you, they sat at the nurse's desk and talked about you. He started thinking about people with formal authority and how they did the same thing. If you weren't loyal to them, it didn't matter how good a nurse you were clinically. He starting thinking why the nasty workers who talked about other employees were allowed to behave that way. He asked his Director and she said, "Sue's a good nurse, she just doesn't get along with people." Ed felt like it didn't matter how good he was at patient care, how good he was with patients and families, it was not about his leadership skills or how good a team player he was...it all boiled down to loyalty to the mob. That's how you get promoted these days and how you keep your job!

Scott (1998) suggested that in bureaucratic organizations loyalty to the norms of the bureaucracy are more important than the product or the customer. Think about it: how often is pleasing the boss more important than doing the right thing? In an organization, people begin to feel that if you are not loyal to those in power, you will not be safe from the alliance and are easy targets for scapegoating and bullying. The

Me?

alliance is the group within an organization who have banded together to seek out people to bully (Hutchison, Vickers, & Jackson, 2006). This is an interesting phenomenon that has received little attention yet appears to be a norm in many healthcare settings (Hutchison, Vickers, & Jackson). Nurses report feeling pressured by the mob to remain silent and avoid being bullied to keep their jobs.

Another function of the mob alliance is to ensure promotions and advancements of those who are loyal. The corruption of the mob becomes embedded throughout the organization's culture as members are promoted. As mobsters climb the organizational ladder they become powerful influences in the ongoing cycle of mobbing and scapegoating. Unfortunately, employees are left feeling lost, powerless, and scared because they have to either become loyal to the mob, or risk losing their jobs.

The Scapegoat Perspective

It has been suggested that *good judgment comes from experience. Experience comes from bad judgments* (Author
Unknown). This is an interesting
suggestion and consistent with how most of us learn through trial and error, failed attempts, and learning through our mistakes.

M ary began to wonder if she was doing something wrong. Bill was not only attacking Mary's performance as a leader, but she also noticed the work wasn't being done. Mary had been working so hard at helping everyone and they seemed more confused than appreciative of her efforts. Mary felt like they weren't working as a team. Maybe they don't know what teamwork really is, she thought. Maybe the other people felt that good teamwork is working individually to do your own part of a project. Mary wondered if maybe she was wrong in thinking that great teamwork is also helping each other with all the parts of a project. Mary remembered that the players on the most effective team she had been on helped each other when their portion was done. They also had healthy dialogues, gave feedback without getting defensive, were committed to

Me? *high quality work, were accountable to each other, and were highly motivated.*

Maybe it's a good learning experience, but at the moment I feel like I'm doing all the work and getting criticized at the same time, by people who aren't doing their work. At the moment I can't see the learning experience for me in understanding team dynamics and being an effective leader.

Bill's criticizing me and he hasn't even handed in his portion. Jane says she doesn't understand what she needs to do. Doesn't Jane know how to read, like the rest of us? If I'm such a lousy leader, why does she keep turning to me for advice? How is it my fault that Bill and Mary couldn't figure out what to do when I did my portion and everything for them so far. Do they want me to just do all their work? I keep having this conversation in my head and going back and forth between thinking I'm doing something wrong versus just being on a lousy team. What confuses me is how do some people know what to do and have turned in their portion of the project, while the other two constantly blame me for everything, when I'm the one trying to help them? Do you think they're just waiting for me to take over and do the work myself again? I'm just so confused and feel alone in this endeavor and thoroughly unappreciated.

Let the Games Begin

Halevy (2008) argued that while team negotiation is a key component of team dynamics and an organizational necessity, competition among team members effectively paralyzes a team's ability to perform. Halevy also suggested that intragroup competition produces higher rates of team conflict and teams that experience conflict consistently lack the ability to complete tasks. Whereas high performing teams consist of members who experience lower levels of conflict and have the ability to successfully negotiate conflict.

Team games are essential components in the team's ability to work towards the team's identified strategy. Team games consist of the internal

Me?

conflict that groups experience (Halevy, 2008) and the concept of individual interests taking precedence over group interests. Halevy described this phenomenon as social conundrum and is the foundation of competition. The level of competition among team members is directly related to the team's ability to be successful. Self-serving interests are essentially a hindrance to team performance and team decision-making capabilities. Therefore, a low performing team will have a high incidence of conflict and high performing team will have a lower incidence of conflict.
Combine a narcissistic leader, a powerful in-group, and team conflict, and the result will most likely reflect an organization that will consistently have high turnover rates, low job satisfaction, poor performance, and constant conflict and chaos.

Summary

In this chapter we began to explore power, politics, and scapegoating as a distraction. Mobbing is a form of scapegoating that is grounded in attempts to gain superiority over others. The unique aspects of scapegoating in healthcare were also explored. In the following chapter we will explore the unique situation when an emerging leader is given formal authority over a group. In these situations the emerging leader is vulnerable to sabotage from the group. Suggestions are provided to minimize the impact.

Me?

Chapter 4 Are You Vulnerable to Being a Scapegoat?

If we are together nothing is impossible. If we are divided, all will fail. Winston Churchill

Sarah's organization was struggling with customer service, declining business, and poor leadership. The organization had been through 3 directors in the last 2 years. Sarah was hired to manage the two departments that were struggling the most. During her interview Sarah was told these departments were the toughest in the organization with a reputation for the poorest customer service, the highest turnover rates, the highest in employee sick call-ins, and the most employee resistance to change. The budgets for these departments were also an ongoing concern where overtime was a constant problem. Department A had issues with excessive overtime. Department B had issues with being at a current deficit of running consistently over budget by more than $100,000 a month. These things needed to be fixed immediately as the organization was losing so much money from these departments it was affecting the entire organization's viability. Sarah was told she would need to focus on these issues immediately upon arrival.

The senior leaders (Vice Presidents) told Sarah they liked her for the role because she would be a change agent, clean house, and fix the budget. They wanted her to fix customer satisfaction and promised to support her in her efforts. Sarah was excited to begin her new job. It was her first real leadership position. She began devising a plan to reduce financial losses, develop realistic fiscally responsible staffing plans, and create an environment where the staff would have input in how they do their jobs. Sarah was appropriately overwhelmed by the number of problems and issues but identified the top 5 things that need to be addressed as:

1. Staffing
2. Sick call-ins
3. Customer service
4. Budget (which should fix itself if the staffing and call-ins are fixed)
5. Communication

Me?

Employees realize that emerging leaders are identified by the formal leaders of the organization as a valuable asset and worthy of promotion. This sort of recognition and support has two results. First, the emerging leader finds encouragement and affirmation that he or she is doing the right thing, so they take on more leadership tasks. Second, the emerging leader's peers may resent the newly promoted leader's special
recognition from higher ups. Higher level leaders may also fear the emerging leader's emergence, especially if others begin to question why the formal leader is not being the agent of change. Eventually, directors and administrators become worried, fear takes over, and the fight for their own survival may change the atmosphere. The dysfunctional leaders begin feeling threatened by the emerging leader and those feelings are often manifested in outward hostility, subtle back-stabbing, and of course scapegoating and mobbing. In the end, the person who demonstrated leadership qualities is not supported by the formal leaders to eventually step into a higher leadership role, but rather is labeled as someone who cannot be promoted, because they create too much disruption in the workforce. The poor scapegoat is left asking, *I thought you wanted me to make changes?* Sounds crazy, eh? Let's get back to Sarah's story.

There were some interesting dynamics in the organization that Sarah didn't appreciate at first. The President was barely visible, and her Vice President was autocratic in her leadership style, ruling with an iron fist and making for a dictatorship-like atmosphere. The Executive Directors where at one time the Directors of the two departments she inherited. The Vice President made it clear to Sarah that the Executive Directors were moved out of the departments Sarah now had because they were not making improvements. Sarah thought it was odd that they were promoted to Executive Directors if they weren't performing effectively in a lower level leadership role. But,

Sarah was new to leadership and thought perhaps she was missing something. Perhaps there was some logic to moving them up and out of the way so real work could be done.

Me?

At first things went well and everyone seemed excited for Sarah to be there. She got feedback from the other Directors and the Executive Directors (whom she reported to) that her skill set was exactly what they needed. They could not wait to see what she would do, what her solutions would be to the challenges they all faced in their own departments. They even said in a meeting, that Sarah was going to save the organization. Sarah felt a pang of something when that was said. Was it a setup? Maybe it was just nerves because they were placing so much hope on her shoulders. Whatever it was, it wasn't a good feeling because to be viewed as the savior of an entire organization was a scary thing and nothing good could come of that? Could it? Maybe? Probably not....

Within 3 months Sarah had begun to make changes in her department. The budgetary crisis slowly improved and both departments began turning a profit. Staffing issues were fixed, the sick call-in rate declined by 80%, vacant positions were filled, and customer service scores were rising steadily each month. Things were appeared great. Sarah was doing all the things she had been hired to do. Changes were happening, employee satisfaction was improving and profits were up. Yet, while Sarah's departments were seeing improvement, the other Directors and Executive Directors started becoming nasty and began bullying Sarah. They started rumors, told the Vice President that Sarah was a loser and listened to complaints from the marginal employees Sarah was pushing to improve. Basically, the other leaders sabotaged Sarah every chance they got. During meetings the Executive Directors pointed out Sarah's department flaws and openly said she had done nothing to improve her areas. Directors discussed the problems they heard about from Sarah's disgruntled employees and questioned why things were not changing. Sarah was shocked. She wondered where this hostility was coming from as she had just provided detailed reports including data showing improvements in both of her departments. She wondered why anecdotal stories seemed to be more important than concrete data.

Sabotaging the Emerging Leader

The ideal situation in functional organizations is to recognize the plight of emerging leaders, and to understand that given the dynamics of change theory a

Me?

change agent will encounter resistance. Kuhn (1996) said that people resist change the more they are tied to the history. Formal leaders need to recognize that pushback is any expected result of change. The formal leader needs to clearly supporting the change agent, rather than allowing the group to shift the focus from their resistance to change, to a focusing on the change agent's leadership style. Scapegoating serves as a distraction from the real work that needs to be done during change creating a dysfunctional environment where young emerging leaders are scapegoated, fail in their role, and eventually leave the organization. Unfortunately the long-term result is nobody wants to take the risk of being a leader and the organization does not make the necessary or intended changes.

Scapegoating on the Rise

It has become commonplace in the United States to avoid accountability and place the blame on someone else. In the 1980s, Ronald Reagan suggested that we needed to reject the notion that every time a law was broken society was guilty rather than the law-breaker. Instead, he suggested that each individual be held accountable for their own actions.

Getting Rid of the Scapegoat

Scapegoating serves the function of creating a momentary illusion that conflict can been reduced through eliminating the scapegoat. For a period of time there is a return of social order in the group by removing the person the group had identified as the source of their problems. However, removal of the scapegoat generates a false sense of security, especially if the group takes on a pattern of blame and looks for another scapegoat the next time a crisis occurs.

When problems occur people often feel the need to place blame on someone. Our politicians blame the woes of society on the other political party, we have lawyers who will defend any of our wrong doings as someone else's

fault, and we have talk show hosts who justify selfish self-centered behaviors as
acceptable behavior.

Me?

Unfortunately, the blame may truly exist in the accusers who need to be accountable for their own behavior. Scapegoating is a common occurrence within every aspect of society. We find it in politics, religion, ethnic groups, organizations, healthcare, and schools. Scapegoating is a form of bullying and very often has the end result of finger pointing, blame, and various forms of violent attacks on someone.

Summary

In this chapter we explored the unique situation when an emerging leader is given formal authority over a group. In these situations the emerging leader is vulnerable to sabotage from the group. Suggestions are provided to minimize the impact. In the next chapter we will explore how arguing is used to avoid accountability. Eventually we watch as an emerging leader is destroyed by scapegoating.

Me?

Chapter 5 What Does it Take to be a Good Team?

Don't argue for other people's weaknesses. Don't argue for your own. When you make a mistake, admit it, correct it, and learn from it, immediately.

Stephen R. Covey

The Mystery of Arguing

Arguing is a great way to avoid having to deal with the real issues. Have you ever gone to an important meeting with a long agenda and the first item on the agenda turns into a huge debate and you never get to the rest of the agenda? It can be redundant, frustrating, and highly unproductive. Patrick Lencioni (2002) described the lack of accountability as one of the five dysfunctions of teams. Maybe everyone is not consciously arguing to avoid accountability, but the result is the same: the argument detracts from the ability of the team to be productive. This dynamic is not unique to meetings, it also occurs in the clinical arena as shown in Figure 1.

Figure 1: Arguing to avoid accountability© (Grossman, 2009).

The scenario in Figure 1 is quite common in the clinical arena; especially as patient care becomes more complicated with numerous specialty clinicians involved and little time to call everyone together to have a team meeting. Lack of accountability can be endemic to an organization (Cohen, 2008). The behavior of arguing becomes part of the culture and is taught to other employees. The best way to avoid these situations is to develop a code of conduct for your team and have clear guidelines for behavior. It is far easier to hold people accountable if you have a set of standards for behavior as show in Figure 2.

Figure 2: Holding co-workers accountable to a code of conduct © (Grossman,

2009)

Without a code of conduct and a previously agreed upon plan, it is difficult to hold co-workers accountable as they have the excuse "we never agreed to that."

Sociologist Eric Hoffer said, *for many people, an excuse is better than an achievement because an achievement, no matter how great, leaves you having to prove yourself again in the future but an excuse can last for life.* This is a sad, but accurate description of interactions in many organizations today.

The Fall of the Emerging Leader

A s time passed the sabotaging of Sarah increased. The Executive Directors pulled her into their office several times a week to sit her down and discuss her progress, or lack thereof. They continued to tell her nobody liked her, she had no team building skills, and she was not bonding with her team. They pointed out all the things she was not doing in an itemized list. Despite all their talk about the importance of data, it was never part of the feedback and when Sarah mentioned her positive data they said data can be manipulated to show
whatever you want. Sarah was devastated. She had no idea this was coming. During this

Me?

time, the Vice President had talked with Sarah, telling her that she was not improving Department B like she should be, and that changes were not occurring. Therefore, they would be taking department B from her and giving her Department C, but she would keep Department A. This was all so confusing to Sarah. Why would they say she was doing nothing in Department B then give her another problem department? This really made no sense.

This latest move of giving her
Department C made the Executive Directors furious. They pulled Sarah in for yet another meeting to explain to her that they felt this decision by the Vice President was wrong and that Sarah should start looking for another job because they would not stand for this. This move for Sarah would take Department C from one of the Executive Directors and she said she would

*not give up her department to Sarah who had no leadership skills. The
Executive Directors began following Sarah around attempting to embarrass
and harass her in front of staff. One Executive Director would show up on
Sarah's departments asking her, "What have you been doing all day?"
"Where have you been?" This behavior by the Executive Director occurred
in front of staff. The Executive Director was so openly hostile it upset the staff
who witnessed it. The bullying and scapegoating became so intense that the
Executive Directors began blaming Sarah for all the organization's issues
and in meetings, they said that since she came, the departments she was
managing were worse, that overall customer service declining for the
organization was her fault, despite her data. They said her departments
positive*

performance was making other people look bad.

*Other Directors started believing the rumors and lies being spread about
Sarah and even said to her that she just wasn't a good fit for the organization
because she wasn't a very strong leader, she was arrogant, overly confident,
and that type of personality didn't match with this organization's mission and
goals. They said Sarah's arrogance was hurting the entire group and the
team could not move forward to perform with her acting like she knew
everything. Some directors admitted that they stayed out of the bullying
conversations about Sarah. Three of them would walk away (hide under the
table) because they liked Sarah but admitted they*

Me?

*saw what was happening and did not want to be next. One Director actually
stood up for Sarah and then began feeling the heat for it so she backed down
in fear of losing her job over it. One Director who Sarah really liked and
viewed as a mentor, said to her in the parking lot one late evening after a
long day of being bullied, that "if they are saying it, it must have some truth
to it". This also devastated Sarah, because she thought she had developed a
relationship with this Director and thought of him as a mentor.*

*Sarah started looking for new job. Sarah was not surprised when the Vice
President called her to her office on a Friday morning for an unannounced
meeting. Sarah new this was coming and she accepted her termination
calmly. Sarah really had nothing to say to the Vice President who sat across
the table very smug talking about leadership skills and that Sarah lacked*

them. Who really lacked the leadership skills here? Not Sarah. Who was the failure in this situation? Not Sarah. But did Sarah feel like the failure. Of course she did.

Vulnerability to Become a Scapegoat

There are certain personality traits common among leaders who emerge in a leaderless group and formal leadership roles, which may make them vulnerable to scapegoating. It has been suggested that a healthy level of narcissism is necessary to being a leader (Brunell, Gentry, Campbell, Hoffman, Kuhnert, & Demarree, 2008). Brunell, et al. described narcissism as a multilevel personality trait where power and exhibitionism are dominant characteristics. Consequently, narcissistic people have a tendency to portray confidence within groups and demonstrate a unique ability to socialize early on in the group. Narcissistic people also develop relationships which bring them attention and a group sense of leadership. Although the group perceives the narcissist as a natural leader and initially supports this person, these personality traits are often destructive over the long-term. The narcissistic leader is initially liked by the group and viewed as a leader but eventually the self-serving personality trait becomes dominant and

Me?

the narcissist destroys the group's ability to perform. In the end, the narcissistic leader's initial favoritism turns to conflict and is no longer favored by the group.

Brunell, et al. (2008) conducted three studies in order to determine the role of narcissism in emerging leadership. The goal of the study was to research whether narcissists are more likely to emerge as leaders among leaderless groups. The results were consistent with the research hypothesis in that narcissism in fact is a predictor for emergent leadership. All three studies indicated that narcissistic personality traits are strong indicators for leadership among groups who have no identified leaders. Furthermore, the authors suggested that narcissistic
characteristics are common among leaders within organizations, however identified a concurrent lack of adequate research in this area.

Nursing Perspective

Group dynamics are essential components in nursing unit structure and stability. Consideration for the emergence of narcissistic leaders within healthcare organizations poses unique leadership problems and overall destructive group dynamics. Consequently, nurses with narcissistic personality traits will rise quickly through the ranks into leadership roles. What does this mean for the health of the organization long-term? Essentially, one may presume the long-term results would be destruction, poor performance, staff dissatisfaction, burnout, and group turmoil among units.

Summary

This chapter began with a review of arguing to avoid accountability. Eventually we watch as the emerging leader is destroyed by scapegoating. In the following chapter we will explore the positive aspects of conflict, a vital stage of team development if handled effectively. Stages of team development, middleness theory, situational leadership, and selfdirected work teams will also be explored.

Me?

Chapter 6 Why Self-Directed Teams Don't Work

**The way a team plays as a whole
determines its success. You may have the greatest bunch of individual stars in the world, but if they don't play together, the club won't be worth a dime.**

Babe Ruth

Conflict is not necessarily a bad thing. All too often we are trying to avoid conflicts when conflict is actually the second phase of a group's stages of reaction to change (Thompson, 2000). The storming stage is actually a point where teams get to the heart of serious discussions and deal with their differing opinions. As long as a team stays in stage one (forming) they will get along, but rarely will anything
meaningful take place. A good example of conflict is the planning of a Christmas party. Teams often think about having a holiday party. Usually the initial thought is it would be nice for everyone to get together around the holidays, socialize in a non-work environment, and bond as a team. During this initial discussion, there is often a lot of enthusiasm as the idea is

formulated. However, as the details are discussed conflict begins to emerge. Is this a Christmas party or a holiday party? Will there be Christmas decorations and Christmas music? What about nonChristian employees? Some people will not want to have a generic, sanitized, politically correct holiday party. What about the cost? Is administration paying for this, or are we paying as employees? How much is it going to cost? How much are people willing to spend?

Me?
Figure 2: Pushing the Tension: Adapted from Thompson 2000, p. 54.

As this debate continues people
begin to withdraw from the discussion and you reach a point where there are less people coming to the party than originally expected. While this contentious
discussion may feel uncomfortable, it is also an opportunity for the leader to reinforce the vision, mission, and values of the team. The leader can remind the team that they are committed to being a team and part of their vision was to do more socializing. This can result in a very meaningful conversation about what people value: the relationship with their peers or having a fancy

party paid for by administration. These types of debates can tear a team apart, or be very healthy if conducted in a safe environment, by a skilled facilitator, who allows everyone to voice their opinion, and avoid namecalling, and judging comments. Good leaders mentor their shared governance council chairs to facilitate these types of discussions.

We had a discussion like this during the economic downturn, when a group we had been working with was told the organization could no longer provide food and beverages for workshops and retreats. The group moved into a frenzied discussion about this and how they felt the administration didn't care about them. Other people thought it was a reasonable budget cut. Finally, someone emerged from the group and said, "I'll take care of it. I will make lasagna for next week's meeting." Someone else said, "I'll bring

Me? beverages."

At the following week's retreat we had the best lunch ever, far better than the box lunches the organization had been providing, and in the process we had grown as a team. People shared recipes. People complemented each other. And people learned how to solve problems on their own, without relying on administration.

This third stage of the process, norming, is where the team adapts to a new set of rules (Thompson, 2000). Teams can easily get stuck in the storming stage or retreat to an even safer zone, but never resolve anything or move forward. If we go back to our Christmas party scenario, teams often abandon all social activities after a failed attempt at a holiday party. Dysfunctional teams (Lencioni, 2003, 2005) can rationalize their behavior by agreeing that socializing is not really necessary, despite the extensive amount of literature that shows socializing is important to teamwork and employee satisfaction (Buckingham & Coffman, 1999; Rath, 2006).

The important lesson is that as a leader you cannot shy away from conflict, and instead should embrace it as a signal that you are discussing a meaningful topic and it is your role as the leader to
encourage that discussion within a controlled environment, where employees feel safe to give feedback.

Being in the Middle

Leaders must always stay focused on doing the right thing morally, ethically, and true to the values of the organization and themselves. By being true to the stated values of the

organization, the leader reinforces those values and sends a clear message to the staff that they *walk the talk* so to speak, and there is a clear connection between the stated values, leader behaviors, and expected employee behaviors, that will be rewarded when it comes to evaluation time. Oshry (1994, 1996) suggested that leaders are inherently caught in the middle between senior leadership

expectations and employee/customer demands. Often to please one is to

Me?

disappoint the other. This is the plight of middle managers and not something that needs to be fixed. It is a source of

frustration for leaders and something that is addressed by finding support from other middle managers and not allowing yourself to be alone and isolated as that can leave you feeling unappreciated.

Situational Leadership

Situational leadership is an

approach based upon the principle that a different leadership approach should be used based upon the employee's level of development with the particular task (Blanchard & Zigarmi, 1999). In nursing, Benner (1984) presented dramatic

research showing how nurses went through distinct stages of clinical development from novice, to advanced beginner, competent, proficient, and expert. Leaders should not get frustrated and revert to authoritative styles for everyone, but customize their approach to the employee's developmental needs.

Perrotto and Grossman (2010) gave examples of how nurses with an interest in leadership can develop their skills through participation in a variety of leadership-like activities in their current role. When an employee takes on a new project such as quality improvement, they may be a novice in that task, despite the fact that they have been an employee for 20 years. For the particular task they are a novice and need direction, as they have no specific experience with the task to fall back on. Without direction the employee may feel as if they were *thrown into the role* and feel uncomfortable to ask for assistance because they assume the leader trusted them to take on the role.

In the second stage of development, the employee begins to feel the frustration of the usual storming stage of group dynamics (see chapter 9). In this stage the employee needs coaching and moral support that they are on track. Resistance from others is normal at this stage of a project. In the third stage, the leader should begin to transfer authority to the employee. They should still provide emotional support but begin asking, *what do you think you should do?* Thus, the employee begins to become comfortable

Me?

with their leadership role, and making decisions on their own. Finally, as the employee gains confidence the leader can delegate full responsibility to the employee, with periodic reporting in. Johnson & Blanchard (1998) also looked at resistance to change in an informative parable that looked at how some
employees easily adapt to change, others take personal responsibility, and others wait for leadership to take care of them.

The challenge of situational
leadership is that most leaders have a set of skills and a leadership style they are most comfortable with and tend to use in most situations, not necessarily based on the employee's needs, but the leaders comfort level. Quinn developed a similar model, The Competing Values
Framework based on a similar approach to customizing the leadership style to the situation (Cameron, & Quinn, 1999). Quinn encouraged the development of a culture, much like shared governance where there are multiple leaders with varied skills. In this approach different leaders can be assigned based on the task and support that is needed. These types of leadership approaches empower staff, provide them with support, and give them the feeling that their input is valued.

Self-Directed Learning Teams

It is common in educational programs to form learning teams where students work on a project to simulate workplace dynamics. LaRue (2004) described action learning as a way for individuals to learn a topic through participation in a team project. LaRue's theory is consistent with Nonaka & Nishiguichi (2001) who suggested that much of learning is tacit: things, which cannot be

described. Action learning when combined with follow-up
discussion provides an opportunity to look at a situation and gain insights,
which can be used in future similar situations. Unfortunately in our
experience students in learning teams often become too focused on getting a
good grade and miss the opportunity to learn about team dynamics.

Sub-leaders often emerge in
learning teams as an ambitious individual
Me?

who conscientiously attempts to keep the group focused on their mission.
Unfortunately this emerging sub-leader puts them self at risk of being
scapegoated at some later point. When the true leader is not fulfilling their
role as a leader, other sub-leaders will step in. The group will often acquiesce
to the substitute leader, as will the defined leader. The sub-leader seizes
control and begins serving as a leader. However, if the sub-leader asserts too
much power or pushes the group too far the group will push back. In general,
groups do not want to over function, they want to maintain their status quo,
which is often less than ideal, but it's
comfortable to be collectively mediocre (that is until the sub-leader comes
along and tips the scales toward quality). Groups react to a high performer
not by emulating them, but by tearing them down or scapegoating them. In
this particular case the typical reaction is to ask, "Who made YOU the boss?"

The scapegoat (emerging leader) reacts by being shocked and wondering
what they did wrong, especially since their motives were honorable: to get
the team to perform. Oshry (1996) suggested that ideally *middles* have a role
of pushing back at the group, if they are going to be successful. However,
middles often allow themselves to become isolated from the group, and in the
process lose their support network, their perspective on the natural group
dynamics, and react to the group's attacks and demands.

United We Stand-Divided We Fall

The social structure of in-groups and out-groups are linked by a sense of a
common identity among group members (Gomez, Dovidio, Huici, Gaertner,
and Cuadrado, 2008). The in-group or more commonly referred to as the
clique, can influence prejudice, bias, stereotyping, and negative feelings
towards members of the out-group. The in-group's ability to interfere with
social acceptance for members within out-groups is a profound characteristic

which can produce both bias and negative outcomes. On the other hand, in-group members who share a common identity with members of the out-group can influence the behaviors

Me?

and perceptions of in-group members by speaking positively towards others.

Groups are powerful influences among social order within organizations, schools, and society, and not so

surprisingly, this power structure has the ability to manipulate a person's acceptance within groups (Gomez, et al., 2008). Intergroup conflict can be attributed to bias and prejudice stemming from in-group members; however conflict and bias can be mitigated through those who identify with superordinate groups. Superordinate groups are unique because they are comprised of people who are neither the in or out group. This group of individuals exist parallel to the in and out group populations. Therefore superordinate groups can have a great deal of influence among the cliques through a shared identity and a

willingness to engage in contact with members of both groups (Gomez, et al.). Essentially, a superordinate group can be beneficial in bridging the gap between the in and out group members.

Divide and Conquer

In-groups and nursing cliques are common among informal social structures in healthcare settings. This component of the informal structure can be both devastating and destructive to unit cohesiveness. Nursing leaders must have the necessary tools in order to address ingroup behaviors while not allowing the behaviors to influence performance reviews and attitudes. Nursing leaders find themselves in difficult situations in units where in-group, or clique, behaviors are strong and influential enough to produce bias, prejudice, and stereotyping.

A combination of narcissistic leaders in the presence of in-groups, along with their destructive behaviors, is a recipe for disaster. In the absence of effective leadership the in-group will silently overcome the unit's informal leadership structure setting the standards for other staff. Consequently, the in-group will effectively demoralize the unit as a whole and eventually chaos will assume a dominant role within the unit's structure.

Me?

Summary

In this chapter we explored the positive aspects of conflict, a vital stage of team development if handled effectively. Stages of team development, middleness theory, situational leadership, and selfdirected work teams were also explored. In the following chapter communication and tools for effective communication when under attack from the group will be covered. Accountability is revisited given our learning's about group dynamics.

Me?

Chapter 7 Communicating When Under Attack

**The single biggest problem in
communication is the illusion that it has taken place.**

George Bernard Shaw

It seems like everybody complains about communication in his or her organization. *They don't tell us anything* seems like the battle-cry from most employees. Yet, when leaders do try to communicate employees argue that they are too busy to attend meetings, or read memos, and they don't like e-mail as it's too impersonal. So, what's a manager to do? There are many factors in effective communication. A leader must assess whether they are using effective communication approaches and whether the complaints of employees are valid or just excuses in avoiding accountability.

Effective Communication Climates

Mehrabian (1981) said that the words accounted for only 7% of communication in volatile situations. The other 93% of communication is the tone (38%) and body language (55%). The argument is often made that face-to-face communication is better because so much of communication is based upon the tone and body language. Far too often leaders blame employees for not reading a memo, an e-mail, a message on the bulletin board, or the policy manual which clearly communicated a certain message.
Employees will argue that they were too busy, missed the message, or failed to appreciate the importance of it. It is not surprising to see the level of

communication difficulties, if only 7% of communication is the actual words. There are two ways to look at Mehrabian's research: Traditionally people argue that you lose something without the body language and tone. Another way to look at it is the body language and tone distract from the message, which is why the words are only providing 7% of the message. Think of why you are reading

Me?

this book? One reason is the book sends a clearer message because you can read it at your own pace, re-read sections you did not understand the first time through, and give the book to your friends to enjoy also. You can't do that with a face-to-face conversation. In fact when you try to convey to others what you were told in a face-to-face conversation portions of the message are often lost or delivered differently than the original messenger.

Tools for Effective Communication

Covey (1990) reported that highly effective people seek first to understand before trying to be understood. Covey's research suggested that highly effective people listen more than they speak to capture information and better understand situations before making decisions. This approach is consistent with how we approach clinical situations where we assess the situation before we prescribe. Unfortunately, in most communication people are too eager to make their point before fully
understanding the other person's perspective. This rush to hasty decisions may also account for the fact that we tend to view most situations as a knowledge deficit that requires further education and training. In reality, 80% of medical errors are caused by communication problems and faulty systems, which are
complicated, and have unnecessary steps that increase the potential for errors (Institute of Medicine, 2000). The most important lesson of effective communication is to listen first, before providing information and solutions.

People are the most valuable resource in a healthcare organization as healthcare is a service industry and it is impossible to take care of the patients without quality staff. Research shows that employees value knowing what is going on and feeling like their voice counts (Buckingham & Coffman, 1999). Good organizations are built on the foundation of good communication and quality staff. It is common for an organization to have a vision of being the number one in their particular field and also being known as the employer of choice. Communicating with employees is a key factor in achieving the mission of any organization.

Me?

Strong leadership and effective communication skills are essential to organizational effectiveness.

Communicating When Under Attack

There are ways to get a team on track if you are not the formal leader. Instead of seizing control you recognize and push the formal leader to do their job. But, what if the leader won't take control? After you become familiar with this concept you realize that being a subleader only has a temporary effect, before it backfires on you and you are labeled as the scapegoat and all of your achievements are reversed out in a protest by the group. So, you stop doing it. You know the definition of insanity is doing something over and over again and thinking it's going to work!

So, how do you prod the true leader? You ask probing, inquisitive, tentative questions of the group. Here's an example of some questions from your particular situation:
1. I'm confused, what is the goal of this project?

2. Can we review again what each person's role is on the project?

3. I just want to verify this, so everyone will have their portion in to the team by Friday night?

4. According to our charter if
anyone's portion is not submitted by Friday at midnight the team leader will reassign their section to another member of the team and move on. Are we REALLY going to do that? Just checking.

Accountability Revisited

Accountability is necessary for any group to be successful. However, when the goals of a group are unclear it becomes easy for the individuals to avoid accountability. One dysfunctional way of avoiding accountability is to shift blame to others for the failings of a group (Cohen, 2008, Lencioni, 2002, 2005). Accountability begins with the formal leader being accountable for their actions and role as a leader. Leaders often live in a subculture where it is acceptable to blame their employees for the shortfalls of the department. Oshry (1996) described *Tops* as individuals playing a role as leader. Tops exist in a sub-culture of acceptable behaviors, which in many organizations include the collective acceptance by fellow Tops that it is acceptable to blame the lack of positive outcomes on their subordinates. There is an implied contract that if I don't hold you accountable as a leader, you won't hold me accountable either.

Oshry described *Middles* as the group caught between the Tops and Bottoms (workers). Middleness is a role at a point in time, not necessarily a formal job title. Middles can be charge nurses, team leaders, project leaders, or the staff nurse caught in the middle between physicians (Top) and patients (family). The role of the Middle is to push the tension in situations by giving the Top constructive feedback of the realities on the front line. While the Middle is also an advocate for the Bottoms, they must remain objective and provide the Bottoms with the reality of the situation.

In our case scenario, Mary pushed back to the bottoms by taking the unpopular stance of reinforcing that research has shown that fatigued nurses have a higher incidence of patient related errors. It might have been easier for Mary to side with the Bottoms in resisting administration's attempts to find a solution to 12-hour shifts. In that case Mary's reaction may have been to join the mob mentality that if administration altered 12-hour shifts in any way the nurses would all quit. Clearly that approach would not help the group to fulfill their initial mission of finding a solution to the problem.

Summary

The focus of this chapter was communication and tools for effective communication when under attack from the group. Accountability was revisited given our learnings about group dynamics. In the following chapter we will explore how to avoid being

scapegoated by developing a wellrehearsed response when asked to be a leader. A plan for documentation and holding others accountable will also be presented.

Chapter 8 Avoiding Scapegoating

Among human beings jealousy ranks distinctly as a weakness; a trademark of small minds; a property of all small minds, yet a property which even the smallest is ashamed of; and when accused of its possession will lyingly deny it and resent the accusation as an insult.

Mark Twain

The foundations of scapegoating are

rooted in jealousy, unclear expectations, and a lack of accountability by team members. Typically, the formal leader abdicates their power and an over functioning member of the group emerges to fill the gap. The emerging leader adds another dimension to an already
complicated situation. The group
passively allows a member to emerge and take charge, to get the tasks done. Over time, the group comes to an appreciation of what the emerging leader has done and resents that the emerging leader is getting credit for the group's success, not asking for enough of the group's input, and doing things differently than they (the group members) would do them. The group is also disappointed with the formal leader for not being a leader. The emerging leader becomes a logical target for the team's displaced anger with the formal leader. Given these dynamics, any approach to avoid scapegoating or minimize the effects must consider the basic causes. Suggestions are listed later in this chapter.

Helping Scapegoats

Being targeted as a scapegoat is similar to other abusive situations. The victim is often left wondering what they did to bring on the attacks. Psychiatrist Judith Orloff (2005) suggested some individuals have intuitive qualities and are especially sensitive to negative energy in their environment. Orloff suggested that people with these tendencies
cultivate an appreciation for the impact of

their environment, avoid negative situations, and focus on placing themselves in positive, supportive situations to avoid stress, fear, and fatigue.

Grant (2013; 2013, April) suggested that the best organizations are comprised of employee's with a giving focus. Giving organization's cultivate effective communication, exhibit teamwork, and employee's support, mentor, and encourage each other's success. Takers, by contrast tend to focus on what's in it for them individually, which does not generally result in a productive, cultivating, and friendly work
environment. Employee's with taker mentalities do not exhibit customer service behaviors and are prone to things like rumors, gossip, and bullying behavior.

Grant was especially concerned about protecting givers from being abused, but they can learn to behave differently with proper mentoring. Gant suggested givers are prone to abuse and should be taught three skills:

1. Separate Generosity From Timidity - Generous people tend not to ask for help, but they will do so if they are acting as agents on behalf of others.

2. Availability -If givers drop everything when anyone asks for a favor, their own productivity suffers. Carve out time and space for uninterrupted work.

3. Empathy -Givers can be easily swayed by emotional appeals for their assistance, but they can make better choices about helping when they are taught to consider others' perspectives in addition to their feelings.

Think Before Over Functioning

Silvia was asked if she would run the annual church fund raising dinner and silent auction this year. She was so honored to be asked that she didn't think about how much work it would be. She wondered why she had been asked, but then thought of all the great ideas she had voiced in the past and realized

Me?
they must have been listening. Her excitement quickly switched from anxiety to panic as she realized she was doing everything herself and everyone, including last years organizer was too busy with kids, work, school, and sick family members. Silvia asked herself why she accepted the role, especially when she got a call one night from the Principal of the school who said people were disappointed in the way things were going. Silvia's immediate response was, "Why didn't they talk to me directly or better yet, why don't they help out?"

Have you ever found yourself being voted the informal leader of a group and thinking why do they keep voting for me? Or, perhaps you're asking the question, why do I keep accepting the role when it is offered. There are several good books on how to say no without feeling guilty (Breitman and Hatch, 2001; Smith, 1985). Often a group of low-performers will avoid assuming responsibility by voting for someone else to be the leader. Interestingly, the person who sends the first email or initiates the dialogue about who should be the team's leader is voted as leader by the rest of the group.

There are a couple of things you can do in these situations to avoid being voted leader if that is your goal. First, don't volunteer to be the leader. It seems simple, but in these situations highperformers generally open dialogue with comments that suggest they wouldn't mind taking on the leadership role. Instead make it clear you are not
volunteering to be the leader, just
suggesting it would be a good idea. Try this line: *I'm wondering if we need a leader for this project to keep us on track. I have too many other projects at the moment to take on the role, but would certainly help someone else if they want to take on the role.*

The second key aspect to avoid being voted as the leader on a team project is to remain silent in the first few hours of team communication. Do not send that first email attempting to clarify

Me?
your understanding of the project. This is a clear bull's eye on your chest for other team members to jump on board and vote you the leader. The point here is that you can learn to choose your battles. One of the things we have learned over the years is that high-performers tend to volunteer to be part of team projects before the project details have even been identified. Why does this happen? Why do highperformers jump up and say "I can help with that project"? High performers want things to be successful and have an internal desire to ensure the projects of their organization are completed. High performers want to be a part of the successes of their organization and they think that by volunteering for projects and doing things themselves they can assure a quality result.

We are not suggesting that you stop volunteering to be on projects and that you avoid informal leadership roles altogether. We are simply suggesting you carefully analyze the projects you are volunteering for and that you wait to see who else is going to be on your team, before stepping forward and taking a leadership role. We often know who the *slackers* in an organization are and these low-performers will either be placed on or will volunteer to be on projects. If you see that Sally and John are on the team and you know from past experiences that Sally and John are low-performers and have had issues in the past meeting deadlines, simply walk away or come up with a good plan to address your

concerns up front through a code of conduct.

Develop a well-rehearsed response for why you cannot manage the project at this time. Pick another project to do because there are always sub-committees and side-projects that need volunteers. Try this response: *Jane, I am so honored that you asked me to lead this project. I have a great deal of respect for you and recognize the importance of this project to the organization's mission. Unfortunately, I am already involved*

Me?
in another big project [describe other project here] and do not think it would be fair at this time to take on something else. Again, I really appreciate your faith in asking me. I am truly honored. I would be happy to help someone else who does take on the role by giving them support and guidance. Thank you again for asking me.

It's Too Late I'm the Leader, Now What?

So, what do you do if you *are* placed on a team where you know from experience of working with members of this group that conflicts will arise, that you may end up doing most of the work, and then get scapegoated? Do you throw in the towel and think, here we go again? But your boss may not like that. Some tips on how to avoid becoming the scapegoat in what appears to be a no win situation are below:

Avoid volunteering to be the project leader. Of course this only works when the boss is not in and can just assign you the role. If your boss assigns you the task it is not a wise move to refuse it. If you can avoid being the project leader, choose your parts of the project based-on your strengths and interests. Do not assume the most complicated parts and the largest parts in anticipation that you will have to do most of the work anyway.

Once you have met *your* deadlines and completed *your* part of the project you wait. This may sound odd but wait for the team to resolve their conflicts. This is a crucial moment for you in the team's ability to manage conflict. What you are waiting for is the team leader to
communicate to the team that deadlines are approaching and people are not performing. This may or may not happen. It is hard to wait and you will want to jump in and assume the role of emerging leader. You may want to re-visit the other chapters where we discussed what happens to the emerging leaders in situations like this. It is a lose-lose

Me?
situation. You are laying the foundation for becoming a scapegoat at this point in time.

As deadlines approach and the work is not done you can do a couple things once you have waited out the leader. You can begin clarifying communication techniques that are outlined in Chapter 7. A good starting point is to send an email clarifying the deadlines and asking if everyone has had an opportunity to review what you have submitted.

Another communication technique is to place a question at the end of each email that asks the group "if there is anything else I can do, let me know". The nice thing about technology today is that e-mails are forever. As you send these clarifying e-mails with offerings to help, it provides you with the documentation you may need later on when the project is late, or the group begins arguing about who did what and who did not meet deadlines.

Document, Document, Document

Documentation is one of our strongest suggestions for communication and effective team building. E-mail trails are the best method for documenting your contributions and the communications among the team. An important part of your communication through e-mail is to never argue, accuse, or attack your teammates. Remain neutral and helpful thus when the arguing, finger pointing, and attacking does begin, you have documented proof that you remained supportive through the whole thing.

Suppose you were appointed as the leader by your supervisor and you have a team made up of mostly *idea* people. *Idea* people are great for offering up ideas about what is wrong, but that is about all they do. Every team has them, and if you are on a team of six people that has two or more *idea* people, it is very likely you will

Me?

struggle with meeting deadlines and accomplishing the team's goals. *Idea* people love to throw a wrench in the team's projects by interjecting ideas in the middle of the project for how they think the project should look and what about this? Did we consider that? *Idea* people are great to have on a team because they can be useful in bringing new ideas to the table, and even offering up great insights on projects that you may not have considered. The problem occurs when the ideas are all they offer, and they continue with their *ideas* late into the project, when the team has already agreed on the goals, tasks, responsibilities, and time lines. The new *ideas* may add little value and delay the team in trying to accomplish their goals. In Chapter 5 we discussed how arguing is a way of avoiding

accountability. Keeping the team on task is one of the emerging leader's key responsibilities and addressing *idea* people can be challenging, but it is necessary to do if goals are going to be met. A good response would be: *Jim, that's a great idea. Can you talk more about how it fits in with our current plan and timelines, so we can decide what to do?*

Encouraging the Team

Another important aspect of the emerging leader's role is to encourage the group. All too often, the group resents the emerging leader and perceives them as receiving all the credit. A great way to avoid that is to offer up praise, especially in public. Another suggestion is if you receive credit for doing a great job leading the group respond by saying, *"A leader is only as good as the team surrounding them. I appreciate the compliment, but I could not do this without my team."* Then give a specific example or two of things they have done to achieve the goals. This is both useful in building cohesiveness and motivating team members into action.

Periodically sending out an e-mail that simply praises the team's efforts and stating how appreciative you are of their

Me?

hard work is usually appreciated. You can also do this in person at team meetings, but our motto is leaving a paper trail. You might be surprised at

how well this works. If you are currently the lead on a project try sending out a praise e-mail and sit back and enjoy the responses you will get from your team. The important thing is to be sincere and not just using this as a tactic. The foundation of all good
relationships is trustworthiness (Covey, 1990) and trust takes time to develop.

Holding the Team Accountable

It is important to remind the team of deadlines, what they agreed to do, and that you do understand how busy they are. We are all busy and a reminder can either be helpful or annoying. You must be careful in how you do this and choose your words wisely. There is an art to giving a gentle reminder that does not come off in an accusatory manner. A couple of things are useful when sending out the: *you are not meeting deadlines*

message. A good place to start is by contacting the people who have not submitted their portion and say, *"I was just getting ready to send out a reminder email about the project and I just wanted to touch base with you. How are you coming along? Is there anything I can do to help? When do you think your portion will be done?"* That information will be useful in constructing your e-mail to the group:

1) Start the message off with praise for the team (avoid individual praise and singling people out)

2) Add in what has been done and the project components that you have received

3) Then add in what parts are still needed (again avoid singling people out and do not mention names)

4) The next part of the email is where you must remain neutral and choose your words carefully. You begin by adding comments about how busy the team members are and how much they have worked

Me?
for this team's project and then say something to the effect of: *I talked with Bob and Sally earlier today and their portions should be done by Friday. I know everyone is busy and I*
appreciate how you have all made this project a priority. If you need any additional assistance please let the team know and we can devise a plan to

assist you.

5) Again thank the team. If you have the leverage to shift deadline by a few days to give people more time, it is greatly appreciated and
indicates that you are listening.

Avoid setting deadlines that leave no room for extensions. Remember when you are setting deadlines for team members to submit their parts of a project you want to leave the team some
breathing room. You cannot set the deadline for Friday afternoon when the project has to be delivered to the
organizational leaders on the following Monday morning at 8:00 am. It is best to have your deadlines be at least a week out from deliverable dates to your boss. This gives you plenty of time to pull the project together and extend deadlines for teammates who are not performing. This also allows you to do additional work on the project if you have a team member who simply is not performing.

Have a Plan and Stick to it

There are three stages to addressing scapegoating: planning, intervention, and follow-up, which are discussed in the recommendations below.

Prevention

1. Be aware of your tendencies to over function, when others are not doing their work.

2. You should think carefully before offering to take charge of a group. While it may seem logical to step forward to get the tasks done, for the good of the group, the long-term effects may be quite different.

3. Do an assessment of the team before volunteering to be the leader: are

Me?
there other people who could be the leader? Will your volunteering to be the leader result in other members take a step back and being less involved? If you do take on the leader role, can you elicit support from the group members to share responsibility for the tasks? Do not try to do it all yourself.

4. Take the time to develop a code of conduct and plan so that it is clear what everyone's roles are

(especially the emerging leader), goals, responsibilities, tasks to be completed, timelines, and any sanctions for people not completing their work.

5. Before agreeing to the role, make sure one last time that everyone agrees and that it is clear what your role will be as the leader.

Implementation Stage

1. Find someone you can trust to objectively observe your performance as an emerging leader and provide feedback to make sure you do not over function in the role and exclude others from the work.

2. Be alert for signs that that the group is abdicating their responsibility and allow you as the emerging leader to over function. Look for warning signs like tasks not being completed, and group members coming up with excuses for not completing their work.

3. Do a re-assessment of your role as the emerging leader. Are you doing what you said you would do? Are you finding yourself doing more than you said you would do? Are there group members who are not fulfilling their role and meeting their obligations? Has anyone emerged who could take on more work?

4. Communicate to the group about how you feel things are going. It is important to be honest at this stage.

Me?
Review the code of conduct and plan to assure that it is still clear what everyone's roles are
(especially the emerging leader), goals, responsibilities, tasks to be completed, timelines, and any sanctions for people not completing their work.

5. Ask the group for honest feedback on your performance as the emerging leader. Make sure everyone still agrees to your role as the leader. If there are concerns address them now. Do not allow yourself to be scapegoated.

Evaluation/Follow up

1. It is important to evaluate the process and outcomes for future learning. Make sure to balance the feedback from your trusted ally or mentor with the feedback from the team. Always remember the team has factors like jealousy, which may affect their ability to provide objective feedback.

2. Review the roles, goals, and
accomplishments. Avoid blaming others for lack of performance, but do make it clear that there were goals and individuals were
responsible to meet them. Be
sympathetic to legitimate excuses, such as a sick family member, but also aware that everyone is busy and effective teams put the team priorities first and find a way to get the work done (Lencioni, 2002, 2005).

3. Do a final re-assessment of your role as the emerging leader. Did you doing what you said you would do? Did circumstances push you to do more than you said you would do? How could you have prevented that? Were there group members who were not fulfilling their role and meeting their obligations? Did anyone else emerge who could have

Me?
taken on more work? Did you encourage others to take on
leadership roles? Is there someone who could have a larger role in the next project?

4. Ask the group for their feedback, preferably through a formal survey. Communicate to the group about how you felt things went. It is important to be honest at this stage. Review the code of conduct and plan, especially everyone's roles, goals, responsibilities, tasks to be completed, timelines, and any sanctions that were needed because people were not completing their work.

5. Finally, ask the group what went well and what areas exist for
improvement on the next project. But, before asking that question anticipate someone being
confrontational and have 2-3 responses of your own prepared in advance. Do not get defensive, but give sincere answers like, "I am sorry you feel that way. My intent was not to hurt anyone or get them in trouble with the boss." If there are any concerns address them immediately. Make sure to make it clear to the group that you did the best job you could under the circumstances and apologize if there is anything you did not accomplish, especially anything that hurt
someone's feelings. Make sure to emphasize your intent was not to be hurtful and you are sorry if it came off that way. Do not allow yourself to be scapegoated! This is a good time to use a mentor for objective balanced

feedback and support.

Summary

The foundations of scapegoating are rooted in jealousy, unclear expectations, and a lack of accountability by team members. In this chapter we discussed how to avoid being scapegoated by

Me?
developing a well-rehearsed response when asked to be a leader. A plan for documentation and holding others accountable was also presented. Below are questions for further consideration before the next chapter, which is on how leaders can help their emerging leaders not to be scapegoated.

Questions for Consideration

1. Given the dynamics of scapegoating what can you do to avoid being perceived as over performing to make your co-workers look bad?

2. Do you have a code of conduct on your team? If you have one, how effective is it? If you don't have one, how could it improve things?

3. Is your team clear on their
performance expectations? Are there any punishments for
scapegoating other employees?

4. What role does the leader play in your organization in allowing bully's to abuse other workers?

5. Does your boss recognize team accomplishments publically? Me?

Chapter 9 What You Can Do as a Leader

**Leadership is the ability to establish standards and manage a creative climate where people are self
motivated toward the mastery of long term constructive goals, in a participatory environment of mutual respect, compatible with personal values.**

Mike Vance

While challenging, there are solutions to scapegoating. The first step is to understand the *storming* nature of group dynamics as a normal stage of development, much like a 2-year-old's temper tantrum or an adolescent's rebellion. Most parents are pretty good at not reacting to a 2-year-old, yet an angry adolescent yelling at you is somewhat harder to accept. Likewise, it is often difficult emotionally for a *Middle* to not take the insults personally, and instead take a step back, and not react to the mob's attacks. Having a support network is essential to survival in the *Middle* role. A mentor, fellow *Middle*, support group, psychosocial profession, or career coach can be an essential ally to understanding the role of a Middle, vulnerability to scapegoating, and ways of creating an effective strategy.

Effective Strategies

There are multiple strategies for dealing with a scapegoating situation. The leader can ignore it, confront it head on, or allow it to play out for the greater good of the team. Gravois (2006) suggested that formal leaders could play a key role in reducing scapegoating behavior early in the process by telling those involved to stop the behaviors. At the risk of
sounding obvious, this really is a simple solution because very often scapegoating behaviors escalate when left unchecked. A simple statement like, *Bob you need to stop attacking your peers because they don't agree with you*, indicates to Bob that these behaviors are unacceptable. This is an example of leading by role modeling and as a leader one of your responsibilities is

Me?

to lead by example and hold your employees accountable. Holding Bob accountable for his attempts to scapegoat his peers will send a message to Bob that his behaviors are not allowed in this organization.

Unfortunately, not all leaders recognize and handle scapegoating and mobbing in a manner that is useful or constructive. Westhues (2002) indicated that managers themselves tend to start the cycle of abuse by feeding on the fears of the majority. It is a simple case of majority rules where vicious gossip and public humiliation take hold of a department and spin wildly out control until someone is victimized. These situations can arise when leaders lack the ability to address mobbing or the leader initiates the mob's attack.

Another dynamic is where the leader is not aware the scapegoating is going on or lacks the moral courage to deal with it. In these situations, scapegoating can reach a point where it is so descructive to the unit that the victim made need to be removed from the situation in order to move forward.

Our own experience is that codes of conduct and team charters that set guidelines for appropriate behavior are the first step to formal leaders holding subordinates responsible for their behavior. One of the benefits of a code of conduct is that everyone on the team has to agree to it at one point in time, hopefully before a crisis takes place. When members start to have difficulties such as bullying, lateral violence, or scapegoating the leader or any individual team member may refer back to the code of conduct without fear of team members arguing that they never heard of the code and did not agree to it.

Depending on how far advanced the attack from the mob is, it may be best for the scapegoat to leave the team in order for the team to move forward. Gerald Ford said that he pardoned Richard Nixon allowing the nation to scapegoat him (Gerald Ford), so that the nation could move forward with more important matters than trying to blame

Me?

and punish Richard Nixon (Woodward, 1999). McKay (2005) explored the stories of famous individuals who had lost their jobs, often as scapegoats for larger organizational issues. Amazingly all of these people found that losing their job proved to be beneficial in the long run, as they moved on to a career that was more fulfilling.

Summary

In this chapter we challenged you to understand scapegoating on a deeper level and begin to explore power, politics, and scapegoating as an predictable aspect of group dynamics that needs attention to avoid the harmful effects. In the following chapter we will explore the unique situation when an emerging leader is given formal authority over a group. In these situations the emerging leader is vulnerable to sabotage from the group. Suggestions are provided to minimize the impact.

Me?

Chapter 10 Toward a Healthier Future

Some people confuse acceptance with apathy, but there's all the difference in the world. Apathy fails to distinguish between what can and

**what cannot be helped; acceptance makes that
distinction. Apathy paralyzes the will-toaction; acceptance frees it by
relieving it of impossible burdens.**

Arthur Gordon

There is little information that addresses leadership and how the lack thereof
is destructive to unit and organizational success. Nurses are hungry for
leaders who demonstrate qualities that provide a sound organizational and
unit based structure. The lack of leadership
responsibility can result in emerging leaders stepping into these roles as they
are driven by an internal need to succeed and have a vested interest in group
success as well. These emerging leaders are often sacrificed as result of their
efforts when failures occur. The failures are inconsequential to the personal
attributes of the informal leader's efforts. These failures, whether big, small,
or catastrophic within the nursing unit or organization will end up circling
back to the emerging leader who kept the failures at bay for as long as
possible. Eventually, the scapegoat stops performing at that high level. The
scapegoat will either leave or become a part of the problem and apathy sets
in. Apathy is a very
dangerous and dark place for an
organization to be in.

Hope on the Horizon

Bullying and scapegoating has been occurring in organizations for decades
(Al-Daraji, 2009). It has taken years for organizations to move beyond
knowing about it to beginning to understand and accept it. The problem
however, is developing a useful and meaningful solution to address it.
Knowing about a problem and accepting that a problem exists are useful in a
couple of ways. First, until someone admits there is a problem there cannot
be a solution. Second,

Me?

acceptance that a solution is needed requires an internal reality check to
evaluate organizational culture. So the question is how does an organization
evaluate its culture? How can you tell if you promote bullying and mobbing?
You could start by asking yourself, do I as a leader protect members of the
mob? Does your organization target and fire

employees who speak out? Have you promoted your friends? These are tough question, and the solution may be even tougher. Al-Darji (2009) said that organizations need to start battling mobbing and bullying by implementing policies that specifically targets these behaviors. While legislation may protect employees from harassment there is no clear direction for mobbing and bullying. Therefore, organizations must take a stance and Al-Daraji suggested adding a no-tolerance policy that includes the protection of employees from
victimization if they speak up. Another solution may be to add policies that define mobbing and bullying with specific guidelines on how to address it. Education of employees and leaders is another crucial component in changing the culture from corruption and collusion to cooperation and cohesion.

Be Proactive Not Inactive

Scapegoating, mobbing, and bullying are like wildfires, you cannot turn your back on them and expect them to put them out. Al-Daraji (2009) said that a proactive approach and early
recognition of bullying is important in creating a better work environment. By being proactive in recognizing bullying you can prevent the situation from turning into mobbing or scapegoating. Also, developing policies that rid your organization of bullying and mobbing should include the input of both employees and leaders. Remember a policy for addressing bullying is only a policy unless it is enforced and useful to those it is intended to protect.

Knowledge IS Power

You may not have the power to stop bullying in your organization. You may be a leader reading this and thinking, wow I never knew about this. You may be

Me?

a leader who knows about it and did not know how to address it. The goal of this book is to give you some insights into what scapegoating is how mobbing and bullying contribute to scapegoating, and what you can do to protect yourself. Whatever your situation, knowledge is the first step towards a solution. By putting a name to the common workplace phenomenon of scapegoating we hope to expose the problem and provide information on workable solutions. The solution may be to develop a plan B and leave your organization (Grossman, 2011). You may have the power to change the culture and you can start by performing an assessment on your organization's current situation. Either way, you now have the knowledge to begin a new chapter in your career.

Me?

Appendix Codes of Conduct

Some people do not like group work, but working in teams is essential to most workplaces. Probably the most dramatic example is research that showed the lack of teamwork in hospitals lead to increased patient deaths (Aiken, Clarke, Sloane, Sochalski, & Silber, 2002). There are very few jobs in your career that won't involve some sort of teamwork. A code of conduct is an essential tool to developing the foundation for teamwork through mutually agreed ground rules that people can be held accountable to. Whether a team is 3 people or 3,000, ground rules are imperative to effective outcomes.

Most people think teams should all think and act the same while. In reality, the key to successful teams is diversity in terms of how people think, where they come from, their previous work
experiences, learning styles, age, and academic background. The differences contribute to teamwork. The key is getting people working together toward a common mission and set of goals, which includes a code of conduct for how people work together to achieve the goals.

Each teams code of conduct should be unique and specific to their circumstances. They key is everyone needs an opportunity for input, if they're going to feel like they own the charter. We could write the *perfect* charter and hand you the template, but if the people don't feel ownership, it's just words on a laminated piece of paper. What we can suggest is your team's code of conduct should address issues like the following story:
Bill works on Unit A and has not been attending all the team meetings. Yesterday he didn't do his portion of a team project. One of his team members questioned the quality of his work as it seemed like it was put together at the last minute. When confronted about this Bill replied, "The problem with YOU people is you're too focused on getting things perfect. I'm

Me?
Administration. What would happen according to your charter?
Some questions to answer in your team charter are in the next section:

Code of Conduct Template

1. Mission/Vision/Values
a. What is the mission of your team? What is your purpose?

b. What is your vision of what success would look like for your team?

c. What behaviors do you value as a team?

2. Team Member Strengths

a. What are the individual strengths of you team
members?

b. What do you enjoy doing as an individual team member that can contribute
to a quality product?

c. Is there a task you would like to work on to develop your personal skills?

3. Goals
a. What are your team goals for the
assignment, group process approach, and quality? b. What are potential
barriers to

the
achievement of your team
goals?
c. State your specific process for
resolution of these potential
barriers.

4. Ground Rules (Make sure to reach consensus on these details).
a. How often will you meet as team?
b. What are the rules for
attendance and participation?

c. Who is in charge of the meetings?

d. How will you communicate between meetings?
e. How will you assign the tasks to be done?
f. How will you keep track of who is doing what?
g. What will be done if a team member does not complete their portion of the assignment deadline, or do not produce the expected quality for their

Me?

portion of the assignment? h. Will there be an assigned team
leader? If yes, what is the role
of the team leader? If there is
no team leader, how will you
handle situations, which
require a leader?
i. What will be done by the team
if a member is not present for
an extended period of time?

5. Conflict Management: You must reach a *consensus* on how you will manage problems.

a. What are the potential conflicts that might arise among or between team members during this course?

b. Specifically, how will team members deal with conflicts? You cannot answer, *we're all adults, we'll deal with it.*

6. Celebrations
a. How will you celebrate your successes?

b. What is your process for providing ongoing positive feedback and support to each other?
c. How will you deal with stress?

Me?

References

Al-Daraji, W. I. (2009). An old problem that keeps re-emerging without a clear solution. *Internet Journal of Law, Healthcare & Ethics, 6*(1).

Armstrong, F. (2002). Blowing the Whistle: The Costs of Speaking Out. *Australian Nursing Journal, 9Australian Nursing Journal, 9* 21.

Bass, B. M. (1990). *Handbook of leadership: Theory, research, & managerial applications (3rd Ed.)*. New York, N.Y.: The Free Press.

Brunell, A. B., Gentry, W. A., Campbell, W. K., Hoffman, B. J., Kuhnert, K. W., & Demarree, K. G. (2008). Leader emergence: The case of the narcissistic leader. *Personality and Social Psychology Bulletin*Social Psychology Bulletin 1676.

Buckingham, M., & Coffman, C. (1999). *First, break all the rules: What the world's greatest managers do differently*. New York, New York: Simon & Schuster.

Center for American Nurses (2008). *Lateral violence and bullying in the workplace*. Crisis Prevention Institute, Inc. (2008). *Alignment: The joint commission leadership standard (LD.03.01.01) addressing disruptive and inappropriate behaviors / The crisis prevention institute's (CPI) workplace bullying seminar*. Retrieved from, www.crisisprevention.com

Cohen, M. H. (2008). *What You Accept is what you teach*. Minneapolis, MN: Creative Health Care Management.

Covey, S. R. (1990). *The 7 habits of highly effective people*. New York, N.Y.: Simon & Schuster.

Eric Hoffer Inspirational Words of Wisdom (n.d.). Quotes about excuses. Retrieved from, http://www.wow4u.com/excuses/ index.html

Gomez, A., Dovidio, J. F., Huici, C., Gaertner, S. L., & Cuadrado, I. (2008). The other side of we: When outgroup members express common identity. *Personality and Social Psychology Bulletin*, 34, 1613-1626.

Grant, A. M. (2013). *Give and Take: A Revolutionary Approach to Success*. New York: Viking Penguin Group.

Grant, A. M. (2013, April). In the Me? Company of Givers and Takers. *Harvard Business Review*, 91(4), 90-97.

Grossman, M. B. (Artist). (2009).

Accountability cartoons.

Grossman, M. B. (2011). *What's Next Create Your Dream Job With a Plan B* (Vol. 1). Bala Cynwyd, PA: Nurse Leadership Builders.

Halevy, N. (2008). Team negotiation: Social, epistemic, economic, and psychological consequences of subgroup conflict. *Personality and Social Psychology Bulletin*Social Psychology Bulletin 1702.

Hoopes, J. (2003). *False Prophets: The gurus who created modern management and why their ideas are bad for business today*. Cambridge, MA: Perseus Publishing.

Hutchinson, M., Vickers, M. H., & Jackson, D. (2006). Like wolves in a pack: Predatory alliances of bullies in nursing. *Journal of Management & Organization, 12*(3), 235-250.

Leff, S. S., Angelucci, J., Goldstein, A. B., Cardaciotto, L., Paskewich, B., & Grossman, M. B. (2007). *Using a participatory action research model to create a school-based intervention program for Relationally Aggressive Girls – The Friend to Friend Program*. M. J. Elias, J. E. Zins, & C. A. Maher (Eds). *Handbook of prevention and intervention in peer harassment, victimization, and bullying*. New York, N.Y.: Hawthorne Press.

Leff, S. S., Crick, N. R., Angelucci, J., Haye, K., Jawad, A. F., Grossman, M. B., & Power, T. J. (2006). Social cognition in context: Validating a cartoon-based attributional measure for urban girls. *Child Development, 77*(5), 1351-1358.

Lencioni, P. M. (2002). *The Five dysfunctions of a team: A leadership fable*. San Francisco, CA: Jossey-Bass.

Lencioni, P. M. (2005). *Overcoming the five dysfunctions of a team a field guide*. San Francisco, CA: Jossey-Bass.

Longo, J. (2007). Horizontal violence among nursing students. *Archives of Psychiatric Nursing, 21*(3), 177-178.

MacKay, H. (2005). *Fired up! : How the best of the best survived and thrived after getting the boot*. New York: Random House Publishing.

Nonaka, I., & Nishiguichi, T. (2001).

Me?

Knowledge emergence. New York: Oxford Press.

Orloff, J. (2005). *Positive Energy: 10 Extraordinary Prescriptions for Transforming Fatigue, Stress, and Fear into Vibrance, Strength, and Love*. New York: Three Rivers Press.

Oshry, B. (1996). *Seeing systems: Unlocking the mysteries of organizational life*. San Francisco: Berrett-Koehler Publishers.

Perrotto, A., & Grossman, M. (2010). Ten ways to the top: Entice the next generation of nurses into leadership positions. *Nursing Management, 41*(4), 28-32.

Rosenbluth, H. (1994). *The customer comes cecond and other secrets of exceptional customer service*. New York, NY: Harper Perenial.

Scott, W. R. (1998). *Organizations: Rational, natural, and open systems (4th ed.)*. Upper Saddle River, NJ: Prentice Hall.

Shakespeare, W. (2009). *Henry IV, Part 2 (Oxford World's Classics)*. New York: Oxford University Press, USA.

Sheridan-Leos, N. (2008). Understanding lateral violence in nursing. *Clinical Journal of Oncology Nursing, 12*(3), 399-403.

The Bible: Authorized King James Version (2008). Leviticus chapter 16. In R. Carroll & S. Prickett (Eds.), *The Bible: authorized King James version*. New York: Oxford Press United States.

Westhues, K. (2002). At the mercy of the mob. *Occupational Health & Safety Canada, 18*(8), 30-34.

Woodward, B. (1999). *Shadow: five presidents and the legacy of Watergate*. New York: Simon & Schuster.

Me?

www.ingramcontent.com/pod-product-compliance
Lightning Source LLC
Chambersburg PA
CBHW030407160726

47992CB00007B/3002